Hot and Cold

Kay Davies
and
Wendy Oldfield

Nov. 28/95

6.⁰⁰

Nelson

Starting Science

Books in the series

Animals
Electricity and Magnetism
Floating and Sinking
Food
Hot and Cold
Information Technology
Light
Local Ecology

Materials
Plants
The Senses
Skeletons and Movement
Sound and Music
Waste
Water
Weather

About this book

Hot and Cold is concerned with the effect of temperature changes on animate and inanimate objects. Children are introduced to the concept of measuring the hotness or coldness of objects and how temperature can affect how things behave. Some cooking is included to illustrate how heat can cause reversible and irreversible changes in different materials. The children learn that heat can travel through different materials, that rubbing objects together produces heat and that hot air rises.

This book provides an introduction to methods in scientific enquiry and recording. The activities and investigations are designed to be straightforward but fun, and flexible according to the abilities of the children.

The main picture and its commentary may be taken as an introduction to the topic or as a focal point for further discussion. Each chapter can form a basis for extended topic work.

Teachers will find that in using this book, they are reinforcing the other core subjects of language and mathematics. Through its topic approach *Hot and Cold* covers aspects of the National Science Curriculum for key stage 1 (levels 1 to 3), for the following Attainment Targets: Exploration of science (AT 1), The variety of life (AT 2), Types and uses of materials (AT 6), Energy (AT 13) and Using light and electromagnetic radiation (AT 15).

First published in 1991 by
Wayland (Publishers) Ltd
61 Western Road, Hove
East Sussex, BN3 1JD, England

© Copyright 1991 Wayland (Publishers) Ltd

Typeset by Kalligraphic Design Ltd, Horley, Surrey
Printed in Italy by Rotolito Lombarda S.p.A., Milan
Bound in Belgium by Casterman S.A.

British Library Cataloguing in Publication Data
Davies, Kay
  Hot and cold. – (Starting science)
  I. Title   II. Oldfield, Wendy   III. Series
  372.3

ISBN 0 7502 0205 X

Book editor: Joanna Housley

Series editor: Cally Chambers

CONTENTS

All the words that first appear in **bold** in the text are explained in the glossary.

The sun is a hot star. It gives the earth light and heat.

HOT SPOT

Stand in the sunshine on a sunny day. Touch your cheeks with your hands. Do they feel hot?

Find lots of things to touch.

Try a window, a car, the playground and your school book.

Do they all feel hot?

Find a shady place outside where you can't see the sun.

Feel your face.

Find lots of things to touch in the shade.

Do they feel hot?

Where would you go if you were feeling cold; in the sun or in the shade?

When we are ill we may have a **fever.** We become too warm. A **thermometer** checks our body **temperature.**

FEVER PITCH

We measure how hot or cold an object is with a thermometer.
Many thermometers use the **Celsius scale**.

They measure between 0° (nought degrees) when ice melts and 100° when water boils. Freezers can get colder than this and ovens much hotter.

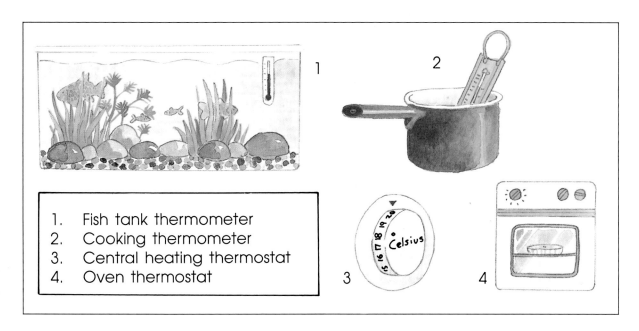

1. Fish tank thermometer
2. Cooking thermometer
3. Central heating thermostat
4. Oven thermostat

We use thermometers to see if machines are working at the right temperature.

A **thermostat** on a machine sets the temperature that is needed.

Look around your home and school.
Can you find thermometers and thermostats?

The dog has been running. It feels very hot.
Panting through its mouth helps cool its body.

HOT DOG

Some animals are warm-blooded.
If the temperature around them changes, they keep their blood at the same temperature.

Hedgehogs are warm-blooded animals.

We are warm-blooded.

Our skin helps us to keep warm or stay cool.
When we are cold we shiver and get goose pimples on our skin. They lift the hairs on our skin.
The hairs trap warm air around our body.

 I'm cold.
I've got goose pimples.

 I'm hot.
I'm sweating.

Run across the playground until you are really warm.
Feel the skin on your forehead.
Sweating water from our bodies helps us cool down.
As it dries on our skin we begin to feel colder.

9

The pike are swimming in the warm summer waters.
When the water is cold in winter they must rest.

COLD FISH

We say some creatures are cold-blooded.

Their blood is not cold but they need the heat from their surroundings to warm their bodies.

When they are warm enough these creatures can be **active**.

They can eat, move and have their babies.

These creatures need warm air or water to be active.
Do you know their names?
Can you find the names of other creatures that are cold-blooded?

In winter when the air and water are cold these creatures don't have the **energy** to move.

PIPING HOT

We burn different **fuels** to give us energy.
We use the energy to keep us warm, cook and run cars.

Fuels like oil, gas and coal are found deep in the earth.

Wind and running water can be used to produce heat too.

We can change heat and energy from all these sources into electricity.
Electricity is easy to use in homes and factories.
How do you heat your home?
Ask your friends. Make a bar chart to show your results.

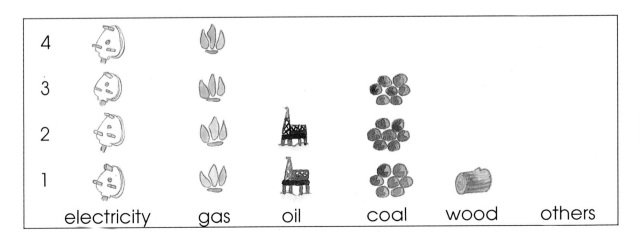

The oil rig's pipes reach the oil under the ocean floor.
Oil is used in homes, factories and machines.

The meat is cooked over a hot fire.
The heat makes it feel, look and taste different.

TASTY AND TENDER

Heat can change things.

Once they are made really hot some things will never be the same again.

Look at a raw potato.
Feel it.
Is it **moist**? Is it hard?

Wrap a potato in foil.
Ask an adult to heat it in the oven for an hour.

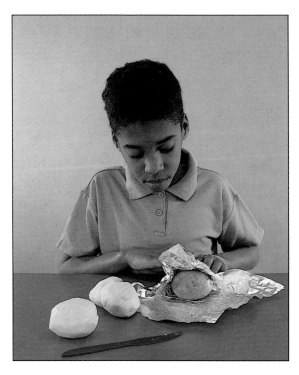

Take the potato out of the foil and cut it in half.

How is it different from your raw potato?

Put a little butter and some salt and pepper on one half of your potato.

Is it nice to eat?

Let the other half go cold. Is it like your raw potato?

MELTS IN THE MOUTH

When some materials are heated they melt and become runny.
When they cool down they harden again.
Runny or hard, the material is still the same.

Collect some chocolate buttons.

Feel one and taste it. Pile the buttons in a dish.
Put it over a radiator or in the sunshine.

What happens to the buttons?
Taste the chocolate.

Put your melted buttons into a fridge.
Can you count them?

Taste them when they are cold.

Do they taste the same?

Does the chocolate feel hard or soft?

The melted chocolate has spread over the girl's face.

The fish have been caught fresh from the sea.
They are kept really cold until they are cooked.

COLD STORAGE

We can make things really cold by putting them in the freezer.
Liquids freeze and become solid.
Liquid in the food freezes and makes the food solid.

Freeze some water in a plastic pot overnight. How is it different from water from the tap?

What happens to the ice when you leave it in a warm place?

Put some cooked peas on to a plate. Feel them.

Put them into a freezer overnight.
Feel them again.

How have they changed?

Drop them into some warm water.
Do peas change at different temperatures?

We need a mat to slide down a big helter-skelter.
It stops our legs from burning.

RUBBING ALONG

When two things rub together they make heat.
Rub your hands together hard. How do they feel?

When metal parts of machines rub together they can become very hot.
The metal can melt.

We use oil to make the parts move more easily.

Put a drop of cooking oil on your hands.

Do they slide more easily when you rub them?

When rough things are rubbed together they get warm very quickly.

Use a sheet of sandpaper to rub some rough wood really smooth.

Can you feel the heat made?

FEELING THE HEAT

Some objects can become hot quickly and easily.
Heat passes through them.
We say they are good **conductors** of heat.

Put some polystyrene, a metal spoon, a plastic ruler, a wooden block and a folded envelope in the icebox of a fridge. Leave them for an hour. Touch them carefully. Those that are good conductors feel really cold. Bad conductors hardly feel cold at all.

Test other things too. Record your findings like this.

	Good conductor	Bad conductor
Polystyrene		*
Metal	*	
Plastic		
Wood		
Paper		
Stone		
Cotton		
Marble		

The metal tray gets very hot in the oven.
We need to wear special gloves to take it out.

Hot air from the burners fills the balloon.
The hot-air balloon can carry people high into the sky.

RISING HIGH

When air is heated it becomes very light.
Hot air drifts upwards because it is lighter than the colder air around it.

Hot-water tanks in our homes are often in cupboards.
Clothes on shelves above the tank are warmed and dried by hot air rising from the tank.

Stick a face on a blown up balloon.

Give your face hair with tissue paper streamers.

Hang the balloon above a warm radiator.

What happens to your balloon face?

How can you stop it dancing?

HOME COMFORTS

We build homes so that they keep us warm in winter and cool in summer.
We choose different materials to help us.
Materials that don't let heat pass through them easily are called **insulators.**

Fill five jars with ice cubes. Wrap each jar with a different material. Try newspaper, foil, cotton wool and string. Leave one unwrapped. Fill five jars with hot water. Wrap these in the same way. Leave all the jars for an hour.

Which materials are good to keep things cold?
Which are good to keep things warm?
Do any keep things warm and cold?

Gloves keep my hands warm in winter.

The ice-cream is wrapped in newspaper to keep it cold.

The hamster chooses dried grasses to build a nest.
The nest keeps it warm and cosy while it is asleep.

Potters can shape the soft clay with their hands.
The clay becomes hard when it is baked in a hot **kiln**.

HOT STUFF

You can make lasting models from this dough. It is baked in an oven to make it hard.
You must get an adult to help you.

Mix together some flour and water until it is so thick that a spoon will stand up in it.
Roll it in your hands.
It should be stretchy, but firm enough to stay in any shape you make.

Divide up the dough and make shapes and models from it.
Ask an adult to bake them in a warm oven for about one hour.
Leave the models to cool.

When your models are cold they will be hard.

Now you can paint them.

GLOSSARY

Active Moving and doing things.

Celsius scale A series of numbers for measuring temperature.

Conductor A material that allows heat to pass through it.

Energy The power to do something.

Fever When an illness makes your body too warm.

Fuel A material that is burnt to provide heat and energy.

Insulator A material that does not let heat pass through easily.

Kiln An oven for baking pottery.

Moist Slightly wet.

Temperature The hotness or coldness of something.

Thermometer An instrument for measuring the hotness or coldness of things.

Thermostat An instrument that keeps a machine working at a fixed temperature.

FINDING OUT MORE

Books to read:

Heat by Bob Graham and Fay J Humphries (Blackie, 1988)
Hot and Cold by Henry Pluckrose (Franklin Watts, 1990)
Snow is Falling by Franklyn M Branley (A & C Black, 1989)
Weather by Kay Davies and Wendy Oldfield (Wayland, 1990)

PICTURE ACKNOWLEDGEMENTS

Tony Stone Worldwide 23; Topham Picture Library 17; Wayland Picture Library 5 both, 14, 18, 20, 28, (Zul Mukhida) cover, 15 both, 16 both, 19 both, 21 both, 22, 25 both, 26, 29 both; Zefa 4, 7, 8, 9, 10, 11 both, 12, 13, 24, 27.
Artwork illustrations by Rebecca Archer.
The publishers would also like to thank St Bernadette's First School, Brighton, East Sussex, for their kind co-operation.

INDEX